We Love

HOLI

Sujatha Menon

First published in Great Britain in 2007 by
Wayland, an imprint of Hachette Children's Books

Hachette Children's Books
338 Euston Road, London NW1 3BH

This paperback edition published in 2010 by Wayland,
a division of Hachette Children's Books.

Produced for Wayland by Q2A Media
Series Editor: Jean Coppendale
Senior Design Manager: Simmi Sikka
Designer: Diksha Khatri
Consultants: Maurice Lyon; Marilyn Bowles

A catalogue record for this book is available from
the British Library.

ISBN 978 0 7502 6209 5

Printed in China

Wayland is a division of Hachette Children's Books,
an Hachette UK Company.
www.hachette.co.uk

The publishers would like to thank the following for
allowing us to reproduce their pictures in this book:

REUTERS: title page, 4, Raj Patidar; 21, Kamal Kishore;
22, Stringer India / Preston Merchant: 5 / Bhaktivedanta Book
Trust International, Inc. www.krishna.com: 6 / Alamy: 7, 10,
ArkReligion.com; 12, Tim Gainey / THE HINDU: 8, 9, 14,
15, 23 / epa: cover, 11, Manjunath Kiran / Stephen Knapp:
13 / His Divine Grace A C Bhaktivedant Swami Prabhupada:
16 / wildphotos.com: 17, Anil Dev / Karun Thakur: 18 /
Lonely Planet Images: 19, Greg Elms / IndiaPicture: 20, 21.

Contents

A shopkeeper in India sells brightly coloured powders, which people throw at each other during Holi.

Hoorah! Holi is here!

Holi is a popular Hindu festival. It is celebrated on the day of the **full Moon** in March.

Hindus celebrate Holi to welcome the arrival of spring. They celebrate with coloured powder and water, music, dance and lots of tasty things to eat.

Children in New York take part in a Holi parade. These parades are popular among Hindu children around the world.

DID YOU KNOW?

On the day of Holi, Hindu farmers offer prayers for a good harvest by roasting grains of wheat in a fire.

Good against evil

Prahlad tells his friends to have faith in God, as He will always help those who believe in Him.

Holi celebrates the victory of good over evil. In Hindu **legend**, there once lived a bad king named Hiranyakashyap, who ordered his people to worship him as God. But his son Prahlad believed in the real God. The king grew angry and told his sister, Holika, to kill Prahlad.

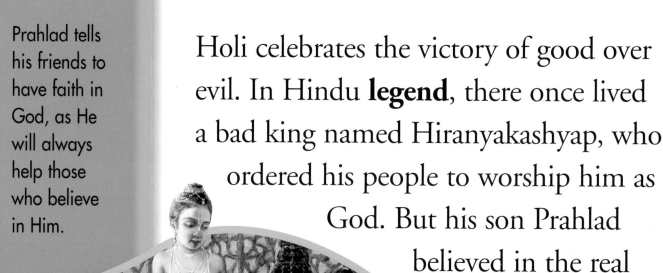

Children in London take part in a play about Holika and Prahlad.

Holika had special powers that stopped her from getting burned, so she sat in a **bonfire** with Prahlad. But God took away her powers because she was using them for evil. Holika died, but Prahlad was saved.

7

Small Holi

Hindus in India prepare to light their street bonfire.

Holi lasts for two days in most countries, except for Nepal, where it is celebrated for a whole week. The first day is called *choti holi* (small Holi). On this day, people clean their houses and collect broken furniture and pieces of wood.

8

At night, people pile up the wood outside their homes and set it on fire.

A dummy figure of Holika is placed in the bonfire to mark the victory of good over evil.

DID YOU KNOW?

In some countries, such as Surinam and Trinidad and Tobago, people burn a castor oil plant instead of lighting bonfires.

Most Hindus
start Holi
celebrations
with a puja,
or prayer.
This puja
is being
held in a
community
centre in
London.

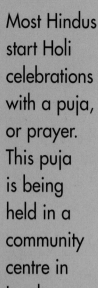

Festival of colours

Everyone waits excitedly for the day after small Holi. This is the day when people from all religions and ages come together to have fun.

People wear old clothes and go out into the streets to throw coloured powder and water at each other. It is very exciting for children as they are allowed to play tricks on the adults.

DID YOU KNOW?

Many Hindus who do not live in India meet in community centres and temples to celebrate Holi.

Covering each other with coloured powder or water is the most enjoyable part of Holi for children.

Holi and Krishna

A young boy dressed as Krishna for Holi. Krishna often played the flute to calm Radha when she was angered by his tricks.

The coloured powder used in Holi also has a story attached to it. It is said that the god Krishna was **jealous** of his good friend Radha, because of her light-coloured skin.

Krishna playing Holi with Radha and her friends.

So one day, Krishna's mother told him to paint Radha's face. Krishna threw coloured powder on Radha and her friends. Now we do this every year.

13

Bathed in colour

Children love to spray coloured water at each other using *pichkari*, or water pistols.

Some Hindus spray coloured water at each other using water pistols. Children throw balloons filled with coloured water.

In other places, coloured powder is mixed in paddling pools. People enjoy taking a dip in these coloured pools.

People have fun throwing coloured water at each other. But the colours mixed in water are difficult to wash off.

15

Some Hindus decorate models of Krishna and Radha with silk clothes and gold jewellery.

In many countries, Holi celebrates the life of Lord Krishna. Hindus in Bangladesh take out figures of Krishna and Radha in a grand **procession**.

16

Mathura, a small city in northern India, is believed to be Krishna's birthplace. Here, Holi celebrations last for two weeks.

People from all over the world come to Mathura during Holi, to join in the celebrations.

DID YOU KNOW?

Some Hindus put up a decorated pole. This is meant to be the tree where Krishna used to hide after playing tricks on Radha.

17

Holi feast

Hindu children in Delhi, India, enjoying a delicious snack of *gujiyas*.

Sweets are a major part of many Indian festivals. On Holi, some Hindu women make a special sweet food called **gujiya**, which is eaten at big family parties.

Thandai is another important part of the celebration. This is a special, flavoured milk with watermelon seeds, almonds, cashew nuts and **cardamom** seeds.

Lots of other delicious foods, such as a flat bread called puri and fried potatoes, are made on Holi.

Along the streets

Holi is celebrated in many different ways by Hindus around the world. Music and dance are a big part of the celebrations both inside and outside India.

The elephant festival in Rajasthan takes place every year during Holi.

In India, people dance in the streets to the beat of the *dhol*, an Indian drum. Colourful parades take place in many big cities.

People wearing traditional clothes dance through the streets of Rajasthan in India.

DID YOU KNOW?

Holi is a holiday which is celebrated in many countries where lots of Hindus live, such as Guyana and Nepal.

A greener Holi

Actors throw flowers during a play about Holi. Many people now throw flowers instead of coloured powder.

Most of the coloured powder used today is harmful to the skin and eyes. So many people have started using different materials.

Some Hindus in India do not burn large bonfires in the streets because this can be dangerous. So instead, they decorate figures of Holika with lights. The lights make the figures look as if they are burning, but are much safer.

A dummy figure of Holika, decorated with lights.

Index and glossary

bonfire a large fire that is built outside by piling up wood

cardamom a herb that is found in India, the seeds of which are added to food to make it taste better

full Moon the day on which we can see the complete disc of the Moon from Earth

gujiya a crescent-shaped Indian sweet food that is filled with grated coconut, raisins and sugar syrup

jealous a feeling of dislike for someone because they have something that we long for

legend a story that is so old that no one knows who first told it

procession a large group of people walking in a line, sometimes singing and dancing to the beat of drums or other instruments